NATIONAL GEOGRAPHIC
Little
Kids™

FIRST BIG BOOK OF DINOSAURS

NATIONAL GEOGRAPHIC

NATIONAL GEOGRAPHIC
Little
kids™

FIRST BIG BOOK OF DINOSAURS

BY CATHERINE D. HUGHES

ILLUSTRATED BY
FRANCO TEMPESTA

NATIONAL
GEOGRAPHIC
WASHINGTON, D.C.

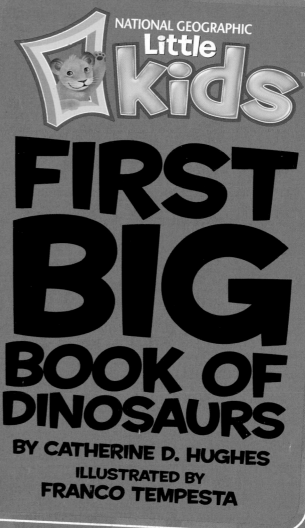

CONTENTS

GIANT DINOSAURS 72

GIGANTIC DINOSAURS 102

HOW TO USE THIS BOOK

Dinosaurs lived on Earth a very long time ago, before there were any people.

SMALL TO GIGANTIC
Dinosaurs came in all sizes. In this book you will find out about 52 small, big, giant, and gigantic dinosaurs. Some were small enough to hold in your hands. Others were bigger than elephants and taller than houses.

DINO FACTS
In each section, look for a drawing that shows the shape and size of the dinosaur. Next to the dinosaur drawing, you will see the figure of a kid who is four feet, six inches tall—about the height of a ten-year-old. That drawing will help you imagine how big that dinosaur was. In the same box, you'll see when the dinosaur lived and what food it ate.

GIANT

AMARGASAURUS HAD A NECK SAIL.

Amargasaurus may have used its **LONG TAIL** like a **WHIP** to **PROTECT** itself from attackers.

This dinosaur's long neck and back were decorated with what looked like a sail. Stiff spines held up *Amargasaurus*'s sail.

No one knows for sure why *Amargasaurus* had the big sail. It might have scared away enemies. Or it may have helped keep the big animal cool.

FACTS

WHEN IT LIVED
early Cretaceous

FOOD
plants

SIZE

84

SAY MY NAME: uh-MARG-uh-SORE-us

WHAT WE KNOW NOW
The text for each dinosaur uses information from scientists who study dinosaurs. These scientists are called paleontologists. This book tells you what paleontologists think now. Some information might change as scientists learn more about dinosaurs.

DINO ART

Because dinosaurs lived so long ago, before there were humans, there are no photographs of them. So an artist drew the dinosaurs you see in this book. The art shows what paleontologists think each dinosaur looked like.

FOR PARENTS

In the back of the book, you will find parent tips for dinosaur games and activities. Also, a world map shows where the fossils of the dinosaurs in this book were found. And finally, a glossary defines words found in the book.

Dig in for a lot more about amazing dinosaurs!

Some of the **SPINES** on the *Amargasaurus* were as **TALL AS A TEN-YEAR-OLD.**

How many dinosaurs do you see in the picture?

85

PRONUNCIATION GUIDE

This line tells you how to sound out the dinosaur's name.

IN THIS CHAPTER
YOU WILL READ ABOUT
15 SMALL DINOSAURS.

SMALL
up to 15 feet long
(5 meters)

BIG
15 to 30 feet long
(5 to 10 meters)

GIANT
30 to 65 feet long
(10 to 25 meters)

GIGANTIC
more than 65 feet long
(25 meters)

Scansoriopteryx
(See pages 24 and 25.)

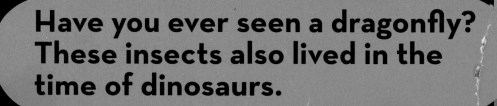

Many **MEAT-EATING** dinosaurs had **FEATHERS**. No dinosaurs had **FUR**.

Have you ever seen a dragonfly? These insects also lived in the time of dinosaurs.

MICRORAPTOR WAS A
FEATHERED GLIDER.

Microraptor weighed less than four pounds. It is the smallest dinosaur in this book.

This little dinosaur had feathers and wings. It did not fly like a bird, but it could glide through the air like a kite.

Microraptor may have used the claws on its feet to climb high up into a tree. Then it leaped off, gliding through the air until it landed on the ground or a branch.

Dinosaurs lived **MILLIONS** of **YEARS AGO**. Dinosaur times are called the **CRETACEOUS, JURASSIC,** and **TRIASSIC.**

FACTS

WHEN IT LIVED
early Cretaceous

FOOD
meat

SIZE

SAY MY NAME: MY-cro-RAP-tore

MICROPACHYCEPHALOSAURUS IS A MYSTERY DINO.

FACTS

WHEN IT LIVED
late Cretaceous

FOOD
plants

SIZE

Scientists know very little about this mysterious dinosaur.

Micropachycephalosaurus may have lived in the forest. It could hide there from bigger animals that might eat it.

This small dinosaur probably sneaked around on the ground, hiding under plants. Maybe it climbed onto tree branches to hide in the leaves.

Micropachycephalosaurus is the **LONGEST** of all dinosaur **NAMES**. But it belongs to one of the **SMALLEST DINOSAURS!**

SAY MY NAME: MY-cro-PACK-ee-SEF-ah-lo-SORE-us

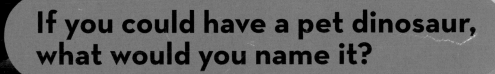

If you could have a pet dinosaur, what would you name it?

Males might have shown their **FANGS TO ENEMIES** to scare them away.

HETERODONTOSAURUS HAD A
TOOTHY MOUTH.

Heterodontosaurus had three different kinds of teeth.

How many kinds of teeth do you have?

The teeth in front of its mouth were small, sharp, and pointed. Those teeth were good for biting leaves.

Heterodontosaurus had bigger, flatter teeth in the back of its mouth. Those teeth were good for chewing.

Males had two long, fanglike teeth on each jaw.

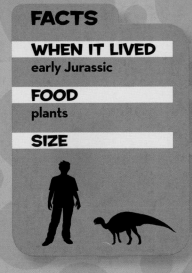

FACTS

WHEN IT LIVED
early Jurassic

FOOD
plants

SIZE

SAY MY NAME: HET-er-oh-DON-toe-SORE-us

OVIRAPTOR WAS A
NESTBUILDER.

Oviraptor looked very much like a bird. It had feathers. Like all dinosaurs, it laid eggs.

Oviraptor made nests for their eggs. They sat on the eggs to protect them.

Parents used their feathered arms to shade their eggs from the bright sun during the day.

FACTS

WHEN IT LIVED
late Cretaceous

FOOD
meat

SIZE

SAY MY NAME: OH-vih-RAP-tore

Oviraptor **DID NOT HAVE TEETH.** These dinosaurs used their strong jaws to **CRUSH FOOD** such as lizards.

Where do you find shade when you play outside?

How many dragonflies can you count in the picture?

COMPSOGNATHUS WAS A
LIZARD HUNTER.

Some dinosaurs hunted other animals. These meat-eaters are called predators. The animals they hunt are called prey.

Compsognathus was a predator. It ran quickly on its two hind legs to catch its prey— lizards, insects, and other small animals.

Compsognathus was about the SIZE OF A TURKEY.

FACTS

WHEN IT LIVED
late Jurassic

FOOD
meat

SIZE

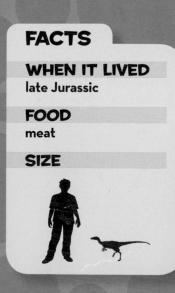

SAY MY NAME: KOMP-sog-NAH-thus

ARCHAEORNITHOMIMUS WAS A
SPEEDY RUNNER.

Archaeornithomimus had long, strong legs. It could run very fast.

Some kinds of dinosaurs ate both meat and plants. Animals that eat both are called omnivores.

This speedy runner was an omnivore. It ate fruit, leaves, eggs, and small animals.

FACTS

WHEN IT LIVED
late Cretaceous

FOOD
meat and plants

SIZE

What is your favorite dinner?

SAY MY NAME: aHR-kee-or-NI-thoh-MIME-us

This **DINOSAUR** had **NO TEETH.**

Can you draw a picture of a dinosaur with bumpy skin?

Some dinosaurs may have lived to be **100 YEARS OLD.**

SCUTELLOSAURUS WAS AN ARMORED DINO.

Scutellosaurus had more than 300 little bumps in its skin. Those bumps were hard little bones.

The bones helped protect the plant-eater. It was as if it had a suit of armor, like a knight.

Scutellosaurus ran on its hind legs. It had a very long tail. The tail helped it balance.

Scutellosaurus was one species, or kind, of dinosaur. Many **SPECIES** of **DINOSAURS** lived at the same time.

FACTS

WHEN IT LIVED
early Jurassic

FOOD
plants

SIZE

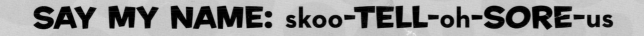

SAY MY NAME: skoo-TELL-oh-SORE-us

SCANSORIOPTERYX WAS A
WINGED CLIMBER.

This tiny dinosaur had feathers and could glide. It had long fingers with strong claws. The claws helped it climb trees.

Up in the treetops, this dinosaur could hunt for insects to eat. Maybe it ate beetles like the one crawling near the *Scansoriopteryx* in the picture.

FACTS

WHEN IT LIVED
early Cretaceous

FOOD
meat

SIZE

Which other dinosaurs in this book could glide? (HINT: Look on pages 10 and 28.)

SAY MY NAME: SCAN-sore-ee-OP-tore-icks

This dinosaur may have used its **CLAWS** to **PULL OUT BUGS** from under tree bark.

PALEONTOLOGISTS are scientists who study **DINOSAURS.**

Paleontologists learn about dinosaurs by **DIGGING** up **BONES, TEETH,** and **FOOTPRINTS** that the dinosaurs left behind.

Have you ever found something while digging in dirt or sand?

PSITTACOSAURUS HAD A PARROT BEAK.

Psittacosaurus did not have any teeth in the front of its mouth. It used its beak like scissors to cut through plants. It did have teeth in the back of its jaws that it used for chewing.

There were dinosaurs on Earth for millions of years. Some kinds, such as *Psittacosaurus*, lived in deserts, where it was very dry. Others lived in forests. Some lived where the weather was hot, and others where it was cold.

Some dinosaur **PARTS** hardened over time and became **FOSSILS**.

FACTS

WHEN IT LIVED
early Cretaceous

FOOD
plants

SIZE

SAY MY NAME: SIT-ah-co-SORE-us

ARCHAEOPTERYX WAS AN EARLY BIRD.

Archaeopteryx is the first bird that paleontologists have found. It was a link, or connection, between dinosaurs and birds.

Archaeopteryx was a dinosaur *and* a bird. Over millions of years, the first birds and all their babies evolved, or changed.

Little by little they began to look more like the birds you see today.

FACTS

WHEN IT LIVED
late Jurassic

FOOD
meat

SIZE

The **BIRDS** you see every day are some of the closest living relatives of the **DINOSAURS.**

SAY MY NAME: ARK-ee-OP-turr-icks

No one knows whether *Archaeopteryx* could actually fly or could only **GLIDE.**

What kinds of birds do you see in your neighborhood?

MANY PLANTS grew where *Minmi* lived.

MINMI WAS A
SLOW MOVER.

Minmi moved slowly. Its tough body was covered with hard armor. It even had armor that grew in the skin on its stomach.

There were **MORE PLANT-EATING** dinosaurs **THAN MEAT-EATING** dinosaurs.

FACTS

WHEN IT LIVED
early Cretaceous

FOOD
plants

SIZE

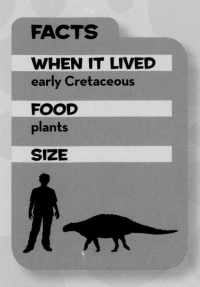

Minmi had small, sharp teeth that it used to bite off the plants it ate. It probably swallowed fruits and seeds whole.

Can you name some fruits that you like to eat?

SAY MY NAME: MIN-mee

BUITRERAPTOR WAS AN INSECT CHASER.

Buitreraptor had small teeth. Its teeth were too small to use for hunting big animals. This dinosaur caught insects, lizards, and other small animals to eat.

Buitreraptor **PROBABLY** used its **LONG, SHARP CLAWS INSTEAD** of its **TEETH** to defend itself.

FACTS

WHEN IT LIVED
late Cretaceous

FOOD
meat

SIZE

Buitreraptor is one of many kinds of dinosaur fossils found in Argentina, South America. Other countries where many dinosaur fossils were found include the United States, Canada, China, Mongolia, Niger, and South Africa.

SAY MY NAME: BWEE-tre-RAP-tore

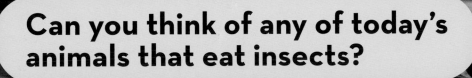

Can you think of any of today's animals that eat insects?

What color would you want
to be if you were a dinosaur?

LEAELLYNASAURA HAD BIG EYES.

This small plant-eater lived near the South Pole, where it was dark and cold part of the year.

Leaellynasaura may have dug burrows to curl up in to stay warm.

Scientists do not know for sure what colors dinosaurs were, but they can make good guesses. They think some dinosaurs may have been very colorful.

Some new species of dinosaurs were **DISCOVERED** by **CHILDREN** who found fossils!

FACTS

WHEN IT LIVED
early Cretaceous

FOOD
plants

SIZE

SAY MY NAME: lee-EL-in-a-SORE-a

HUAYANGOSAURUS HAD A SPIKY BACK.

The pointy spikes on *Huayangosaurus*'s body may have been protection against predators. The two big spikes on its back might have stopped taller meat-eaters from biting this dinosaur.

Huayangosaurus also had flatter spikes, called plates, that grew along its whole back.

Large **MEAT-EATING DINOSAURS LIVED** at the **SAME TIME** as this **SPIKY-BACKED PLANT-EATER.**

FACTS

WHEN IT LIVED
middle Jurassic

FOOD
plants

SIZE

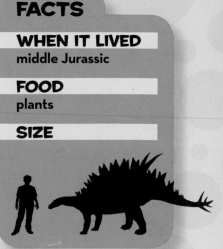

SAY MY NAME: hwah-YANG-oh-SORE-us

Flying reptiles called **PTEROSAURS** (TER-uh-sores) **LIVED IN THE TIME** of dinosaurs.

Can you find three pterosaurs flying near this *Huayangosaurus*?

Struthiomimus means **"OSTRICH MIMIC."** This dinosaur looks a little like an ostrich.

Have you ever seen an ostrich?

STRUTHIOMIMUS WAS QUICK ON ITS FEET.

Struthiomimus was one of the fastest runners of all dinosaurs. Its legs were long and strong. It ran faster than any human.

The dinosaur had a small head and a long neck and tail. Its stiff tail helped *Struthiomimus* keep its balance as it ran.

Scientists think *Struthiomimus* was omnivorous. It may have eaten plants as well as small animals such as lizards.

FACTS

WHEN IT LIVED
late Cretaceous

FOOD
meat and plants

SIZE

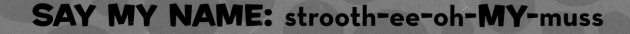

SAY MY NAME: strooth-ee-oh-MY-muss

39

IN THIS CHAPTER
YOU WILL READ ABOUT
15 BIG DINOSAURS.

SMALL
up to 15 feet long
(5 meters)

BIG
15 to 30 feet long
(5 to 10 meters)

GIANT
30 to 65 feet long
(10 to 25 meters)

GIGANTIC
more than 65 feet long
(25 meters)

Triceratops
(See pages 54 and 55.)

40

BIG

NO dinosaurs **LIVED** in the **WATER.** But some dinosaurs were **GOOD SWIMMERS.**

PENTACERATOPS HAD A
HORNED HEAD.

This dinosaur had five horns sticking out of its head. Two stuck out over its eyes. A third horn grew on top of its nose.

A frill stretched between two other horns on top of its head. Short spikes grew all along the frill. The frill helped the dinosaur show off to other *Pentaceratops*.

FACTS

WHEN IT LIVED
late Cretaceous

FOOD
plants

SIZE

Do you like to swim?

SAY MY NAME: PEN-ta-SER-ah-tops

HERRERASAURUS HAD A
BIG MOUTH.

Herrerasaurus **WALKED** on its **HIND LEGS.**

This fierce meat-eater could open its mouth very wide. Its strong jaws slid back and forth and chomped down hard. Its big mouth held a lot of strong teeth.

Herrerasaurus was one of the earliest big meat-eaters. It lived in the Triassic, the beginning of the time of dinosaurs.

FACTS

WHEN IT LIVED
late Triassic

FOOD
meat

SIZE

SAY MY NAME: huh-RARE-ah-SORE-us

Herrerasaurus used its **TEETH** to cut prey into **CHUNKS** it could **SWALLOW.**

What do you use your teeth for?

Does the horn on this dinosaur's nose remind you of a rhinoceros?

STYRACOSAURUS HAD A FANCY FACE.

Styracosaurus used its **SHARP BEAK** to **CHOP OFF** the **PLANTS** it ate.

A big horn on its nose, spikes along its frill, and knobs on its cheeks gave this dinosaur an unusual look.

Paleontologists have found many fossil skeletons of these dinosaurs together. They think *Styracosaurus* traveled in groups.

FACTS

WHEN IT LIVED
late Cretaceous

FOOD
plants

SIZE

SAY MY NAME: sty-RACK-oh-SORE-us

UTAHRAPTOR HAD
CLAWED FEET.

Utahraptor had POWERFUL LEGS.

This dinosaur had scary-looking feet! When *Utahraptor* attacked, it leaped up in the air. Then it kicked hard. The big sharp claws on its feet stabbed its prey.

The claws on its feet were about 12 inches (30 centimeters) long. That is longer than the cover of this book.

Utahraptor also had a lot of sharp teeth. Like many small meat-eaters, this dinosaur was smart, fast, and dangerous.

FACTS

WHEN IT LIVED
early Cretaceous

FOOD
meat

SIZE

SAY MY NAME: YOO-tah-RAP-tore

Can you jump and kick like *Utahraptor?* Try it outside.

Paleontologists found this **DINOSAUR'S FOSSILS** in **UTAH,** in the United States. That is how it **GOT THE NAME** *Utahraptor.*

ANTARCTICA is a very **COLD PLACE TODAY.** But when *Cryolophosaurus* lived there, Antarctica **WAS MUCH WARMER.**

CRYOLOPHOSAURUS HAD A PRETTY CREST.

The crest on the top of *Cryolophosaurus*'s head was bony. Two little horns grew on each side. The decoration may have made the dinosaur attractive to other *Cryolophosaurus*.

FACTS

WHEN IT LIVED
early Jurassic

FOOD
meat

SIZE

What do you do to make yourself look nice for a party?

Paleontologists found this toothy dinosaur's fossils near the South Pole. It is one of the first dinosaurs to be discovered on the continent of Antarctica.

SAY MY NAME: CRY-oh-LOW-fo-SORE-us

NOTHRONYCHUS HAD
CLAWED ARMS.

FACTS

WHEN IT LIVED
middle Cretaceous

FOOD
plants

SIZE

This plant-eater had huge claws on its hands. It used these claws to grab branches. *Nothronychus* had a beak and more than 100 tiny teeth.

You can see a giant relative of *Nothronychus* called *Therizinosaurus*, on page 90. They lived at different times and in different places.

There are at least **1,000 SPECIES** of dinosaurs.

SAY MY NAME: noh-THRON-ih-cuss

Can you point to the bird flying in the forest near the dinosaur?

Triceratops had about **800 SMALL TEETH.** The plant-eater used them to **CUT UP** the **TOUGH PLANTS** it ate.

FACTS

WHEN IT LIVED
late Cretaceous

FOOD
plants

SIZE

TRICERATOPS HAD
THREE HORNS.

The horns on its head and the frill around its neck were used to show off to other *Triceratops*. The dinosaurs sometimes used their horns to fight each other, too.

Triceratops means **"THREE-HORNED FACE."**

Paleontologists found the fossils of three young *Triceratops* together. This makes them think that these dinosaurs traveled in family groups.

Can you point to the three horns on this *Triceratops* fossil?

SAY MY NAME: tri-**SERR**-ah-tops

55

MUTTABURRASAURUS HAD A
BUMPY NOSE.

No one knows exactly why *Muttaburrasaurus* had a big bump on its skull. It was right behind the holes in its nose, called nostrils.

Scientists often make a GOOD GUESS, called a HYPOTHESIS, to answer things they do not know for sure.

Here are three hypotheses about this dinosaur's odd nose.

FACTS

WHEN IT LIVED
early Cretaceous

FOOD
plants

SIZE

It might have helped *Muttaburrasaurus* smell things better, look more attractive to a mate, or make its calls louder.

SAY MY NAME: mutt-ah-**BUHR**-ah-**SORE**-us

Nobody knows for sure what **SOUNDS DINOSAURS MADE.**

What is your hypothesis about what this dinosaur sounded like?

FOSSILS of *Europasaurus* were **FOUND** in **GERMANY**, a country on the continent of **EUROPE**.

EUROPASAURUS WAS AN
ISLAND DINO.

This dinosaur was smaller than its relatives. *Europasaurus* is closely related to *Apatosaurus* (see page 106) and *Brachiosaurus* (see page 108).

Europasaurus looked a lot like those gigantic dinosaurs, but it did not grow as big. It lived in forests on islands, small bits of land surrounded by water.

FACTS

WHEN IT LIVED
late Jurassic

FOOD
plants

SIZE

Can you draw a picture of an island?

SAY MY NAME: yoo-**ROPE**-ah-**SORE**-us

OURANOSAURUS HAD A
BACK SAIL.

The **BIG CREST** along this dinosaur's whole back looked a bit like the **SAIL** on a **SAILBOAT.**

Ouranosaurus lived in a rainy place where the land often flooded.

The dinosaur had plenty of plants to eat. But when the land flooded, *Ouranosaurus* had to watch out for gigantic crocodiles, which lived in the time of dinosaurs.

Have you ever seen a crocodile at the zoo?

SAY MY NAME: oo-RAHN-oh-SORE-us

FACTS

WHEN IT LIVED
early Cretaceous

FOOD
plants

SIZE

Can you see better with one eye open or with both eyes open?

CARNOTAURUS HAD A SQUARE HEAD.

This dinosaur might remind you of a bull because it had two horns on its head. The odd-looking dinosaur had a very small lower jaw. Its head was shaped like a square.

Some dinosaurs couldn't see in front of them with both eyes at the same time. But *Carnotaurus*'s eyes were far enough forward on its face that it could see ahead with both eyes at once.

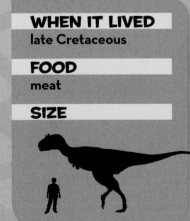

Carnotaurus had **TINY ARMS.** They were so small that the **MEAT-EATER** could not use them to do much.

FACTS

WHEN IT LIVED
late Cretaceous

FOOD
meat

SIZE

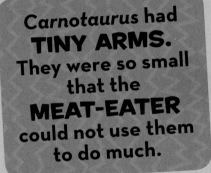

SAY MY NAME: KAR-no-TORE-us

STEGOSAURUS HAD A SPIKED TAIL.

Huge spikes on *Stegosaurus*'s tail were a good weapon. If a predator threatened it, *Stegosaurus* could swing its big tail and smack the enemy with the spikes.

Stegosaurus was the **BIGGEST SPECIES** of plate-backed plant-eaters.

Stegosaurus also had tall plates sticking up from its back. Another dinosaur in this book had tall plates, too. Do you remember *Huayangosaurus* on page 36?

FACTS

WHEN IT LIVED
late Jurassic

FOOD
plants

SIZE

SAY MY NAME: STEG-oh-SORE-us

The **PLATES** helped keep **MEAT-EATERS** from **ATTACKING** *Stegosaurus.*

How many plates do you see on the *Stegosaurus* that is closest to you?

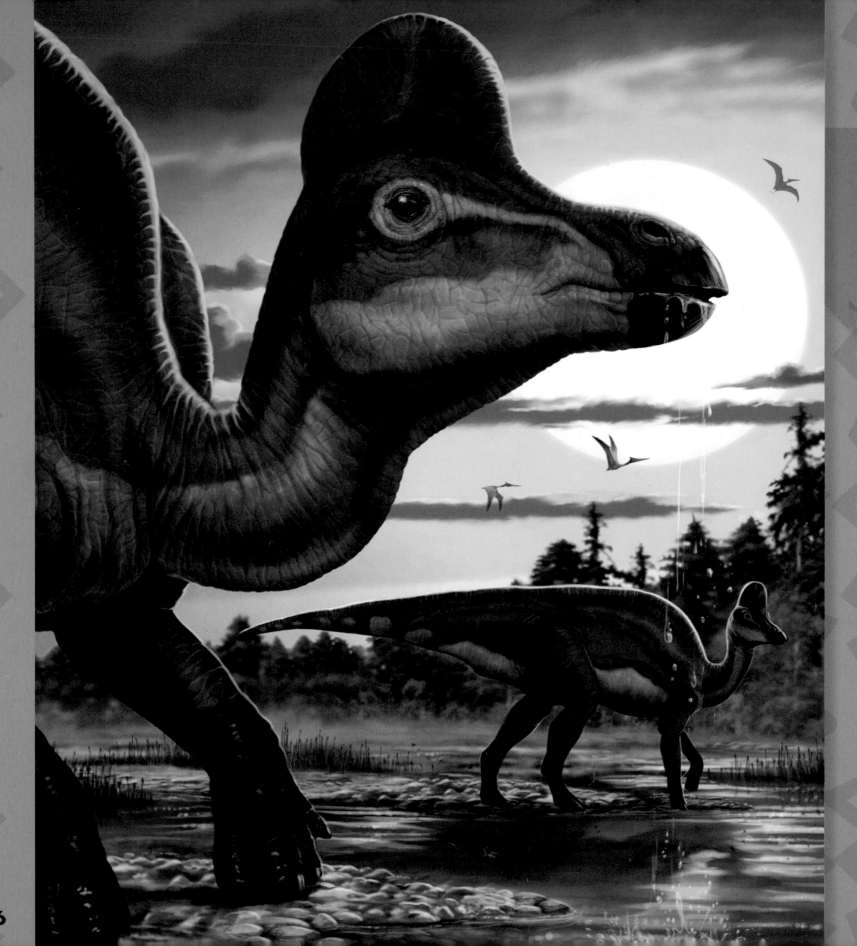

CORYTHOSAURUS HAD A HELMET HEAD.

Corythosaurus was one of several related species of dinosaurs called crested duckbills.

These dinosaurs lived in **GROUPS** called **HERDS.**

FACTS

WHEN IT LIVED
late Cretaceous

FOOD
plants

SIZE

When *Corythosaurus* breathed in, the air traveled from its nose up through the crest on its head. Its crest may have made the dinosaur's sounds louder.

Do you have a soft voice and a loud voice? Say "Corythosaurus" both ways!

SAY MY NAME: co-**RITH**-oh-**SORE**-us

PLATEOSAURUS WAS A LEAF CHOMPER.

Paleontologists have FOUND more than 100 SKELETONS of this kind of dinosaur.

At the time *Plateosaurus* lived, it was one of the biggest dinosaurs.

It had a lot of teeth for ripping leaves off trees.

If *Plateosaurus* wanted to eat leaves that were high in a tree, the dinosaur could stand on its hind legs to reach them. It may have used its arms to pull down branches.

SAY MY NAME: PLAT-ee-oh-SORE-us

What do you do if you can't reach something you want?

Sometimes dinosaurs **FOUGHT EACH OTHER** to see which one was **STRONGER.**

70

PACHYCEPHALOSAURUS HAD A THICK HEAD.

Pachycephalosaurus had a very hard head. These dinosaurs may have used their heads to whack each other's sides.

Pachycephalosaurus ate **LEAVES, SEEDS,** and **FRUIT.**

FACTS

WHEN IT LIVED
late Cretaceous

FOOD
plants

SIZE

Some dinosaurs fought each other to guard the area where they wanted to live. They did not always like to share their space.

Can you name three things that you are good about sharing?

SAY MY NAME: pack-ee-**SEF**-ah-lo-**SORE**-us

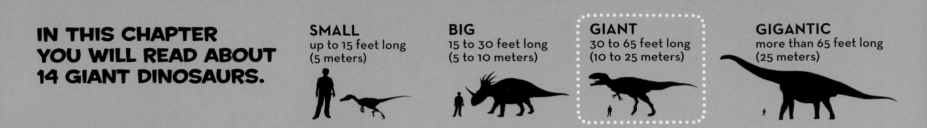

IN THIS CHAPTER YOU WILL READ ABOUT 14 GIANT DINOSAURS.

SMALL
up to 15 feet long
(5 meters)

BIG
15 to 30 feet long
(5 to 10 meters)

GIANT
30 to 65 feet long
(10 to 25 meters)

GIGANTIC
more than 65 feet long
(25 meters)

Tyrannosaurus

(See pages 100 and 101.)

GIANT

73

Mother *Maiasaura* **BROUGHT FOOD** to their **BABIES** while they were still **IN THE NEST.**

MAIASAURA WAS A GOOD MOTHER.

Like all dinosaurs, *Maiasaura* laid eggs. Most meat-eaters' eggs were long and thin. Plant-eaters like *Maiasaura* laid rounder eggs.

These dinosaurs were too big to sit on their eggs to keep them warm. Instead, *Maiasaura* mothers covered their eggs with leaves.

FACTS

WHEN IT LIVED
late Cretaceous

FOOD
plants

SIZE

Where do your mom and dad get food to bring home?

SAY MY NAME: MA-ya-SORE-a

IGUANODON HAD
SPIKED HANDS.

Iguanodon had spikes on its hands. The spikes were in the place where thumbs might be, but were actually part of the dinosaur's wrist bones.

Iguanodon may have used its "thumbs" to stab a predator if it attacked.

FACTS

WHEN IT LIVED
early Cretaceous

FOOD
plants

SIZE

What do your thumbs help you do?

Iguanodon had three **STRONG FINGERS** and a **LONG LITTLE** finger.

SAY MY NAME: ig-'WAN-oh-don

The first **FLOWERING PLANTS** appeared at about the same time that *Iguanodon* lived.

The **TAIL** of the *Ankylosaurus* had a **HARD, BONY CLUB** on the end of it.

If you were an *Ankylosaurus*, would you rather face a giant crocodile or a *Tyrannosaurus*?

ANKYLOSAURUS HAD AN
ARMORED BODY.

Ankylosaurus had a strong body covered in tough armor. This dinosaur moved slowly. It did not run away from trouble. It depended on its hard body for protection. Even its eyelids were covered with armor.

A *Tyrannosaurus,* such as the one in the picture at left, would have had a hard time biting the armored *Ankylosaurus.* (You can read more about *Tyrannosaurus* on page 100.)

When facing an **ENEMY** such as a giant crocodile, *Ankylosaurus* could use its **HEAVY TAIL** to **HIT** the **ATTACKER.**

FACTS

WHEN IT LIVED
late Cretaceous

FOOD
plants

SIZE

SAY MY NAME: AN-kee-lo-SORE-us

79

TSINTAOSAURUS HAD A UNICORN SKULL.

Tsintaosaurus had a long bone that stuck out from its forehead, making it look a bit like a unicorn. But unicorns are make-believe. *Tsintaosaurus* was real.

Can you think of other make-believe creatures?

Paleontologists had to find more than one fossil skull before they were convinced that the long bone really grew from the dinosaur's forehead.

FACTS

WHEN IT LIVED
late Cretaceous

FOOD
plants

SIZE

SAY MY NAME: sin-tau-**SORE**-us

Tsintaosaurus **HORNS** may have been a **DECORATION** that made the dinosaurs attractive to each other.

Can you name some healthy green things that you eat?

LESSEMSAURUS WAS A
BIG EATER.

Big dinosaurs ate big meals. *Lessemsaurus* had to eat a lot of plants like the cycads it is eating in the picture.

As you know, there are no more dinosaurs like *Lessemsaurus*. But did you know that there were dinosaurs on Earth for about 160,000,000 (160 million) years?

That is such a long time it is almost impossible to imagine!

FACTS

WHEN IT LIVED
late Triassic

FOOD
plants

SIZE

Lessemsaurus was named for **DINO EXPERT** Don Lessem, who has written more than 40 books about dinosaurs.

SAY MY NAME: LES-em-SORE-us

AMARGASAURUS HAD A NECK SAIL.

Amargasaurus may have used its **LONG TAIL** like a **WHIP** to **PROTECT** itself from attackers.

FACTS

WHEN IT LIVED
early Cretaceous

FOOD
plants

SIZE

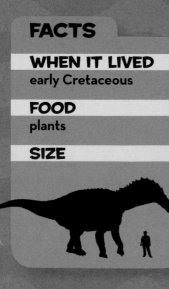

This dinosaur's long neck and back were decorated with what looked like a sail. Stiff spines held up *Amargasaurus*'s sail.

No one knows for sure why *Amargasaurus* had the big sail. It might have scared away enemies. Or it may have helped keep the big animal cool.

SAY MY NAME: uh-MARG-uh-SORE-us

84

Some of the **SPINES** on the *Amargasaurus* were as **TALL AS A TEN-YEAR-OLD.**

How many dinosaurs do you see in the picture?

Can you find the small lizard in the picture?

86

RIOJASAURUS WAS THE FIRST GIANT DINO.

This giant dinosaur was one of the first really big plant-eaters. It had a long, thin neck and tail. Its body and legs were heavy.

Smaller dinosaurs could walk on two legs. But *Riojasaurus* walked on all four legs. The giant and gigantic dinosaurs had to walk on four legs because two legs could not hold up all their weight.

Many dinosaur **NAMES** end in *"saurus."* **SAURUS** means **LIZARD.**

FACTS

WHEN IT LIVED
late Triassic

FOOD
plants

SIZE

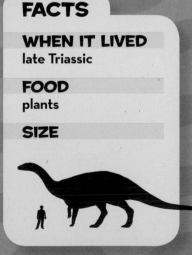

SAY MY NAME: REE-oh-hah-SORE-us

YANGCHUANOSAURUS WAS A SCARY DINO.

Yangchuanosaurus was so powerful it could kill prey much larger than itself.

One of the dinosaurs that had to watch out for this meat-eater was the gigantic *Mamenchisaurus*, which you can see on page 111. The two dinosaurs lived in the same place at the same time.

A construction **WORKER** in **CHINA** found the first skeleton of *Yangchuanosaurus* while digging to **BUILD A DAM.**

FACTS

WHEN IT LIVED
late Jurassic

FOOD
meat

SIZE

Do you think this dinosaur looks scary?

SAY MY NAME: YANG-chew-an-oh-SORE-us

BIG TEETH and BIG CLAWS made *Yangchuanosaurus* a GREAT PREDATOR.

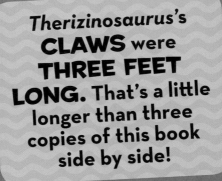

Therizinosaurus's **CLAWS** were **THREE FEET LONG.** That's a little longer than three copies of this book side by side!

THERIZINOSAURUS HAD
HUGE CLAWS.

Even though this dinosaur had huge claws, *Therizinosaurus* was not a meat-eating predator. It was a plant-eater.

It also may have eaten insects such as ants and beetles. Its big claws would have been handy for digging in the ground to find insects.

FACTS

WHEN IT LIVED
late Cretaceous

FOOD
plants and insects

SIZE

Have you ever tried digging in dirt to find an earthworm?

SAY MY NAME: THERE-ih-ZIN-oh-SORE-us

ACROCANTHOSAURUS HAD
EYE RIDGES.

Acrocanthosaurus had **38 SHARP TEETH** in its upper jaw.

FACTS

WHEN IT LIVED
early Cretaceous

FOOD
meat

SIZE

Acrocanthosaurus peered out of eyes that had bony ridges around them.

This dinosaur had very strong muscles in its neck and back.

Acrocanthosaurus was one of the biggest meat-eating dinosaurs. It was not a fast runner. But it was powerful and could kill prey bigger than itself.

SAY MY NAME: ACK-ro-CAN-tho-SORE-us

Acrocanthosaurus **HUNTED** other kinds of dinosaurs, like the one in the background, for **DINNER!**

If you were a dinosaur, would you rather be a plant-eater or a meat-eater?

The **SPINES** on *Spinosaurus's* back reached **SEVEN FEET HIGH**—taller than almost any human.

How many pterosaurs do you see flying in the sky in the picture?

SPINOSAURUS HAD A LONG JAW.

Spinosaurus had a long jaw like a crocodile's. It caught fish to eat.

FACTS

WHEN IT LIVED
late Cretaceous

FOOD
meat

SIZE

Do you remember *Amargasaurus* from page 84? It looked a little like *Spinosaurus*. They both had long spines and sails on their backs.

This dinosaur was a meat-eater; *Amargasaurus* was a plant-eater. The two dinosaurs didn't live at the same time. *Spinosaurus* lived later.

SAY MY NAME: SPINE-oh-SORE-us

EDMONTOSAURUS WAS A HERD TRAVELER.

Every year *Edmontosaurus* traveled long distances to find food. This kind of travel is called migration. *Edmontosaurus* migrated in large herds.

What is the farthest you have traveled from home?

Edmontosaurus herds walked more than **1,000 MILES** a year. It would take a whole day and night to go that far in a car.

Edmontosaurus had hundreds of diamond-shaped teeth. It used its teeth to grind the tough plants it ate.

SAY MY NAME: ed-MON-toh-SORE-us

FACTS

WHEN IT LIVED
late Cretaceous

FOOD
plants

SIZE

In this picture, pterosaurs **SWOOP UNDER** the *Shunosaurus's* **LONG TAIL.**

SHUNOSAURUS HAD A
CLUB TAIL.

There was a bony lump on the end of *Shunosaurus*'s tail. The huge dinosaur could swing its tail and hit enemies with the hard end.

Can you name three animals you have seen that have tails?

Workers digging in China found the fossils of several entire *Shunosaurus* in one place. Finding a whole fossilized dinosaur is rare.

FACTS

WHEN IT LIVED
middle Jurassic

FOOD
plants

SIZE

SAY MY NAME : SHOO-noh-SORE-us

TYRANNOSAURUS WAS THE
DINOSAUR KING.

Tyrannosaurus is one of the most famous dinosaurs. It was a fierce hunter with long, sharp teeth.

The jaws of the *Tyrannosaurus* were very strong. The dinosaur could use its jaws to crush animals it caught for food.

FACTS

WHEN IT LIVED
late Cretaceous

FOOD
meat

SIZE

Can you think of another animal that is a fierce hunter?

Tyrannosaurus could have **GULPED** down some **SMALL DINOSAURS** without even chewing.

SAY MY NAME: tye-RAN-oh-SORE-us

Tyrannosaurus's **TEETH** were the size of **BANANAS.**

SMALL
up to 15 feet long
(5 meters)

BIG
15 to 30 feet long
(5 to 10 meters)

GIANT
30 to 65 feet long
(10 to 25 meters)

GIGANTIC
more than 65 feet long
(25 meters)

Brachiosaurus
(See pages 108 and 109.)

GIGANTIC

103

This gigantic dinosaur **LIVED** in the **FOREST.**

REBBACHISAURUS WAS AN AFRICAN GIANT.

This gigantic dinosaur lived in Africa. It had a big ridge, or long bump, on its back.

The ridge may have helped the dinosaur cool off.

Fresh air and breezes could reach all the skin covering the long ridge. That could help a hot dino cool down!

How do you cool off when you get too hot?

The biggest dinosaurs were plant-eaters. They had **SMALL BRAINS** about the **SIZE** of two **CHICKEN EGGS.**

FACTS

WHEN IT LIVED
late Cretaceous

FOOD
plants

SIZE

SAY MY NAME: re-BACK-eh-SORE-us

APATOSAURUS WAS A GOOD PROTECTOR.

Long ago some paleontologists thought they had found the fossils of a new dinosaur. They named it *Brontosaurus*.

Years later, other paleontologists realized that the *"Brontosaurus"* fossils were really those of a dinosaur that already had a name: *Apatosaurus*.

So there never really was a dinosaur called *Brontosaurus*.

FACTS

WHEN IT LIVED
late Jurassic

FOOD
plants

SIZE

Did anyone ever call you by the wrong name?

SAY MY NAME: uh-**PAT**-uh-**SORE**-us

Traveling in herds, *Apatosaurus* may have protected **YOUNG DINOSAURS** by keeping them in the **MIDDLE OF THE GROUP.**

FACTS

WHEN IT LIVED
late Jurassic

FOOD
plants

SIZE

BRACHIOSAURUS WAS A
TREETOP EATER.

Brachiosaurus had a very long neck. Its front legs were longer than its back legs.

The dinosaur's long neck and front legs helped it reach leaves growing high up in trees.

This tall dinosaur was **HEAVY.** It **WEIGHED** more than **12 ELEPHANTS.**

How much do you weigh?

Brachiosaurus walked very slowly and could not run.

SAY MY NAME: BRACK-ee-oh-SORE-us

MAMENCHISAURUS HAD A
LONG NECK.

This dinosaur had the longest neck of any animal that ever lived. Its neck was as long as five or six giraffe necks!

Mamenchisaurus didn't have to walk around much to keep eating. It could stand in one spot and sweep its head back and forth to reach plenty of leaves.

FACTS

WHEN IT LIVED
late Jurassic

FOOD
plants

SIZE

Stretch your arm up a wall while standing on tiptoe. Who in your family can reach the highest?

SAY MY NAME: mah-MEHN-chee-SORE-us

The neck on this dinosaur was almost as **LONG AS ITS BODY AND TAIL** put together.

Have you ever seen a dog wag its tail to show that it is happy?

DIPLODOCUS HAD A WHIPLIKE TAIL.

Diplodocus's tail was longer than any other dinosaur's.

Diplodocus had LONG, SKINNY TEETH.

FACTS

WHEN IT LIVED
Triassic to middle Jurassic

FOOD
plants

SIZE

Some paleontologists used to think that when it snapped its long tail like a whip, the noise scared away predators.

Now they think that *Diplodocus* actually used its tail to signal, or "talk" to, other dinosaurs.

SAY MY NAME: dih-PLOD-uh-kus

NUROSAURUS WAS A DESERT DISCOVERY.

The **FOSSIL SKELETON** of *Nurosaurus* was discovered in 1990.

Nurosaurus fossils were found in a desert in China. It was long and heavy—the biggest dinosaur in the area at the time it lived.

Dinosaurs disappeared about 65 million years ago. Scientists think that a big asteroid—a huge rock from space—hit the Earth. It made big clouds of dust and smoke that changed the weather, killing almost all the dinosaurs.

SAY MY NAME: NEW-ro-SORE-us

Have you ever been to a desert?

FACTS

WHEN IT LIVED
early Cretaceous

FOOD
plants

SIZE

There was only **ONE DINOSAUR** known to be **BIGGER** than *Paralititan*. You'll see it when you turn the page.

PARALITITAN WAS A MANGROVE DINO.

Paralititan lived in mangrove forests near the edge of an ocean. Mangroves are trees that grow where it is very wet. Mangrove forests are filled with these trees and many other plants.

Living there meant that this plant-eater had plenty to eat. It needed to eat hundreds of pounds of food every day.

What is the biggest animal you have ever seen?

FACTS

WHEN IT LIVED
late Cretaceous

FOOD
plants

SIZE

The **WET FOREST** where *Paralititan* lived millions of years ago is now a **HUGE DESERT**.

SAY MY NAME: pah-ral-e-**TIE**-tan

ARGENTINOSAURUS WAS A
HEAVYWEIGHT.

Some dinosaurs were as long as this dinosaur. A few were taller. But *Argentinosaurus* may have been the heaviest. It weighed about the same as 20 elephants.

Araucarian **TREES**—which *Argentinosaurus* ate so long ago— **STILL GROW** in **ARGENTINA,** South America.

FACTS

WHEN IT LIVED
late Cretaceous

FOOD
plants

SIZE

Paleontologists have only found fossils of a few *Argentinosaurus* bones. But they know enough about dinosaurs to figure out what the whole dinosaur probably looked like.

SAY MY NAME: ahr-gen-**TEEN**-oh-**SORE**-us

Argentinosaurus was the **LARGEST** known animal that **EVER LIVED ON LAND.**

If you were a dinosaur, which dinosaur in this book would you want to be?

PARENT TIPS

Extend your child's experience beyond the pages of this book. A visit to a natural history museum's dinosaur exhibit is one great way to continue satisfying your child's curiosity about dinosaurs. Take this book along with you to see how many dinosaurs featured here are on exhibit at the museum. Here are some other activities you can do with *National Geographic Little Kids First Big Book of Dinosaurs.*

SIZE UP DINOSAURS (MATH)

The dinosaurs in this book are categorized according to size: small, big, giant, and gigantic. Compare the lengths of one dinosaur from each chapter to your child's length (lying down). Mark a starting line. Have your child lie down with her feet at the line. Mark her length. Then, from that same starting line, use a measuring tape and help her measure and mark the sizes of *Micropachycephalosaurus* (2 feet/.6 meters long), *Cryolophosaurus* (20 feet/6 meters long), *Riojasaurus* (36 feet/11 meters long), and *Diplodocus* (90 feet/27 meters long). Bonus idea: Have your child count how many of her lengths equal each dinosaur's length.

CREATE A TIME LINE (TIME)

"Millions of years ago" is a hard concept for adults to grasp, much less for kids who are learning to picture last year, this year, and next year. Have your child draw a simple time line to help him get a picture of the Triassic, Jurassic, and Cretaceous periods. Label Triassic at the left, Jurassic in the middle, and Cretaceous at the right. Draw an arrow on the right end of the line and label it so that it points to "today." Pointing to the line, explain that the Cretaceous was a long time ago (145 to 65 million years ago); the Jurassic was even longer ago (200 to 145 mya); and the Triassic was the longest ago (250 to 200 mya). Compare to yesterday, last week, and last month.

BUILD A HIDING PLACE (IMAGINATION)

Grab a couple of high-back chairs and a big bedsheet or blanket. Pretend that a time machine took you and your child back to the time of the dinosaurs. You're hidden from the dinosaurs inside a blind, so that you can make observations without being detected. Ask your child to tell you what she sees, then tell her what you see, and continue taking turns building a story about your time with the dinosaurs. When you've exhausted your imaginations, time-travel back to the present and draw pictures of what you saw.

DINOSAUR EGG HUNT (SEARCH STRATEGIES)

Make dinosaur eggs using papier-mâché (find directions online). Place a toy or treat inside each egg before sealing. Hide the eggs around the house or yard. Have your child invite a few friends over and have a dinosaur egg hunt. When the children find all the eggs, have them break the eggs open to find the treats.

NAME THAT DINO (ALPHABET)

Have your child write the alphabet down the side of a big sheet of paper. Then go through this book and have your child identify the first letter of each dinosaur's name. Have him make a check mark next to the corresponding letter on his alphabet. If he's still interested in the game, have him make up new dinosaur names that begin with each of the letters without a check mark.

WATCHING DINOSAURS (OBSERVING)

Birds, by some definitions, are dinosaurs (see page 28). Attract "dinosaurs" to your backyard by setting up a "dinosaur feeder" (bird feeder). Sit with your child and watch the birds (they tend to be most active in early morning and late afternoon). Make a chart that lists the most common visitors to your feeder along the side and the days of the week along the top. Each day, have your child mark off the species of living dinosaurs that stop by for a visit.

DINOSAUR DIET (CATEGORIZING)

Some dinosaurs were plant-eaters, others meat-eaters, and a few were omnivores. Have your child decide which dinosaur diet he wants for dinner. Take him to the grocery store to buy the ingredients for a plant (vegetarian) or omnivorous (meat and vegetables) meal. Let him pick from among fruits, vegetables, and meats as you discuss how fruits and vegetables grow and which animals different meats come from.

DIGGING FOR DINOS
(MOTOR SKILLS)

Pretend to be paleontologists digging for fossils. Using ten cleaned and boiled chicken bones, make a dinosaur dig at home. Bury the bones at various levels in dirt in the yard, in a sandbox, or in sand placed in a big container. Using a toy shovel and a couple different sizes of paintbrushes, have your child dig carefully to find the ten "fossils" you've buried.

MAKE A DINOSAUR
(CRAFTS and SHAPES)

Using colored construction paper, cut out several shapes—squares, ovals, triangles, circles, and rectangles—of various sizes. Your child can make pictures of dinosaurs by gluing the shapes onto a sheet of construction paper. For example, use a big circle to make the body, rectangles as legs, two triangles as open jaws, and tiny triangles as teeth.

DINO JOKES
(HUMOR)

Goofy jokes are great for giggles. Search online for dinosaur jokes or make up your own. Encourage your child to make up a few, too. Here are three to get you started:

Q: How can you tell there's an *Apatosaurus* in your refrigerator?
A: The door won't close!

Q: Which dinosaur could jump higher than a house?
A: All of them. Houses can't jump!

Q: What did *Triceratops* sit on?
A: Its tricera-bottom.

DINOSAUR GAMES
(PLAY)

Play a variation of duck, duck, goose by having your child and his friends call out dinosaur names instead: e.g. *"Apatosaurus, Apatosaurus, Tyrannosaurus!"* Play a variation of tag by pretending that the person who is "it" is a meat-eating dinosaur and the other players are prey. Play hide-and-seek, pretending that the seeker is a hunter and the others are prey.

DINOSAURS ONLINE
(BONUS MATERIAL)

Go online to print dinosaur cards! kids.nationalgeographic.com/kids/animals/creature feature/

DINOSAUR MAP

Use this world map to see where fossils of the dinosaurs in this book were found.

ARCTIC

NORTH AMERICA

ATLANTIC OCEAN

PACIFIC OCEAN

SOUTH AMERICA

ATLANTIC OCEAN

NORTH AMERICA

Scutellosaurus
Struthiomimus
Pentaceratops
Styracosaurus
Utahraptor
Nothronychus
Triceratops
Stegosaurus
Corythosaurus
Pachycephalosaurus
Maiasaura
Iguanodon
Ankylosaurus
Acrocanthosaurus
Edmontosaurus
Tyrannosaurus
Apatosaurus
Brachiosaurus
Diplodocus

SOUTH AMERICA

Buitreraptor
Herrerasaurus
Carnotaurus
Lessemsaurus
Amargasaurus
Riojasaurus
Argentinosaurus

ANTARCTICA

Cryolophosaurus

EUROPE
Compsognathus
Archaeopteryx
Europasaurus
Plateosaurus
Iguanodon
Rebbachisaurus

ASIA
Microraptor
Micropachycephalosaurus
Oviraptor
Archaeornithomimus
Scansoriopteryx
Psittacosaurus
Huayangosaurus
Iguanodon
Tsintaosaurus
Yangchuanosaurus
Therizinosaurus
Shunosaurus
Mamenchisaurus
Nurosaurus

AFRICA
Heterodontosaurus
Ouranosaurus
Iguanodon
Spinosaurus
Rebbachisaurus
Paralititan

AUSTRALIA
Minmi
Leaellynasaura
Muttaburrasaurus

OCEAN

EUROPE

ASIA

AFRICA

PACIFIC
OCEAN

INDIAN
OCEAN

AUSTRALIA

ANTARCTICA

GLOSSARY

CLAW
a sharp nail on an animal's foot or hand that is usually curved and slender

CONTINENT
one of seven large land divisions on Earth: North America, South America, Europe, Asia, Africa, Australia, and Antarctica

CRETACEOUS
the period of time from 145 to 65 million years ago. Most dinosaurs were extinct at the end of this period.

DESERT
a dry area of land that receives ten inches or less of rain each year

DRAGONFLY
any of several species of large insect with a long, slender body and two pairs of narrow wings

EXTINCT
no longer existing

FANG
a long, sharp tooth

FLOOD
overflowing of a body of water such as a river that spills onto normally dry land

FOSSIL
a preserved part or trace of an ancient animal or plant

FRILL
a feature around the neck of an animal that was, in the case of dinosaurs, made of either bone or cartilage

HERD
a group of animals that live together

HYPOTHESIS
an unproven explanation or assumption that needs further investigation or testing

ISLAND
a piece of land that is surrounded by water and is smaller than a continent

JURASSIC
the period of time from 200 to 145 million years ago

MANGROVE
a tree with very long roots that is native to tropical coastlines

MIGRATE
to move from one place to another regularly

OMNIVORE
an animal that eats both meat and plants

OSTRICH

a big, fast, flightless bird that lives in Africa. It is the largest bird alive today.

PALEONTOLOGIST

a scientist who studies dinosaurs and other extinct animals and their habitats

PREDATOR

an animal that hunts other animals (prey) for food

PREY

an animal that a predator hunts and kills for food

PTEROSAUR

an extinct flying reptile

SKELETON

the stiff structure, made of bone or cartilage, that supports the body's soft tissues and organs

SOUTH POLE

the southernmost point on Earth, located on the continent of Antarctica

SPECIES

a category, or kind, of animal or plant

TRIASSIC

the period of time from 250 to 200 million years ago

INDEX

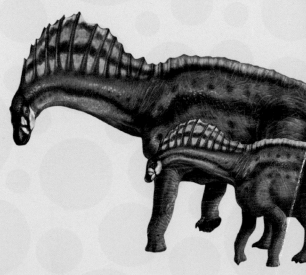

Published by the National Geographic Society

John M. Fahey, Jr.,
Chairman of the Board and Chief Executive Office

Timothy T. Kelly,
President

Declan Moore,
Executive Vice President; President, Publishing

Melina Gerosa Bellows,
Executive Vice President;
Chief Creative Officer, Books, Kids, and Family

Prepared by the Book Division

Nancy Laties Feresten,
Senior Vice President, Editor in Chief, Children's Books

Jonathan Halling,
Design Director, Books and Children's Publishing

Jay Sumner,
Director of Photography, Children's Publishing

Jennifer Emmett,
Editorial Director, Children's Books

Carl Mehler,
Director of Maps

R. Gary Colbert,
Production Director

Jennifer A. Thornton,
Managing Editor

Staff for This Book

Robin Terry, *Project Manager*
Catherine D. Hughes, *Project Editor*
David M. Seager, *Art Director*
Lori Epstein, *Senior Illustrations Editor*
Ruthie Thompson, *Designer*
Wanda Jones, Ph.D., *Research*
Kate Olesin, *Editorial Assistant*
Kathryn Robbins, *Design Production Assistant*
Hillary Moloney, *Illustrations Assistant*
Grace Hill, *Associate Managing Editor*
Lewis R. Bassford, *Production Manager*
Susan Borke, *Legal and Business Affairs*

Manufacturing and Quality Management

Christopher A. Liedel, *Chief Financial Officer*
Phillip L. Schlosser, *Senior Vice President*
Chris Brown, *Technical Director*
Nicole Elliott, *Manager*
Rachel Faulise, *Manager*
Robert L. Barr, *Manager*

For Jack and Christopher, the loves of my life, and for little kids
everywhere, whose perpetual curiosity inspires me every day.
A special thanks to Stephanie Hughes, Aline Alexander Newman,
Mary Ann Teitelbaum, and Jennifer Kirkpatrick Zicht for their
invaluable help with this book.   **–C.D.H.**

A special thanks to paleontologist Rodolfo Coria, Ph.D., of Neuquén, Argentina,
for being so generous with his time and expertise in the creation of this book.

Acknowledgments

Matthew F. Bonnan, Ph.D., Dept. of Biological Sciences, Western Illinois University

Brooks B. Britt, Dept. of Geology, Brigham Young University

Robin Cuthbertson, University of Calgary

Andrew A. Farke, Ph.D., Curator of Paleontology, Raymond M. Alf Museum of Paleontology

Catherine A. Forster, Ph.D., Dept. of Biological Sciences, The George Washington University

Thomas R. Holtz, Jr., Ph.D., Dept. of Geology, University of Maryland

Dr. John "Jack" Horner, Curator of Paleontology, Museum of the Rockies

James I. Kirkland, Ph.D., Utah Geological Survey

Kevin Padian, Ph.D., Museum of Paleontology, University of California, Berkeley

Thomas H. Rich, Ph.D., Curator of Vertebrate Paleontology, Museum Victoria

Alex Tirabasso, Canadian Museum of Nature

John A. Whitlock, Ph.D., University of Michigan Museum of Paleontology

Xu Xing, Ph.D., Institute of Vertebrate Paleontology and Paleoanthropology,
Chinese Academy of Sciences

Professor Fucheng Zhang, Institute of Vertebrate Paleontology and Paleoanthropology,
Chinese Academy of Sciences

Photo Credits
p. 55, Francois Gohier/Photo Researchers Inc.; p. 68, Mervyn Rees/Alamy

The National Geographic Society is one of the world's largest nonprofit scientific and
educational organizations. Founded in 1888 to "increase and diffuse geographic knowledge,"
the Society works to inspire people to care about the planet. National Geographic reflects
the world through its magazines, television programs, films, music and radio, books, DVDs,
maps, exhibitions, live events, school publishing programs, interactive media and merchandise.
National Geographic magazine, the Society's official journal, published in English and 33 local-language
editions, is read by more than 38 million people each month. The National Geographic Channel reaches
320 million households in 34 languages in 166 countries. National Geographic Digital Media receives more
than 15 million visitors a month. National Geographic has funded more than 9,400 scientific research,
conservation and exploration projects and supports an education program promoting geography literacy.
For more information, visit nationalgeographic.com.

For more information, please call 1-800-NGS LINE (647-5463) or write to the following address:
National Geographic Society, 1145 17th Street N.W., Washington, D.C. 20036-4688 U.S.A.
Visit us online at www.nationalgeographic.com/books

For librarians and teachers: ngchildrensbooks.org

More for kids from National Geographic: kids.nationalgeographic.com

For information about special discounts for bulk purchases, please contact National Geographic Books
Special Sales: ngspecsales@ngs.org

For rights or permissions inquiries, please contact National Geographic Books Subsidiary Rights:
ngbookrights@ngs.org

ISBN: 978-1-4263-0846-8 (hardcover)
ISBN: 978-1-4263-0847-5 (library binding)

Printed in China

12/TS/2